HOW LIFE BEGAN

By Melvin Berger

Illustrated by
Jerry Lofaro

Doubleday
New York London Toronto Sydney Auckland

For Benjamin with love from his *Zeyde*

PUBLISHED BY DOUBLEDAY
a division of Bantam Doubleday Dell
Publishing Group, Inc., 666 Fifth Avenue,
New York, New York 10103

DOUBLEDAY and the portrayal of an anchor
with a dolphin are trademarks of Doubleday,
a division of Bantam Doubleday Dell
Publishing Group, Inc.

The author and the publisher would like to
thank Dr. Ian Tattersall of the American
Museum of Natural History for his careful
review of the manuscript and illustrations
for this book.

Library of Congress Cataloging-in-
Publication Data
Berger, Melvin
    How life began / by Melvin Berger.
      p.   cm.
    Summary: Explores the mysteries of how
life began, discussing the formation of
planet earth, the first signs of living
matter, the time of dinosaurs, and the
development of human beings.
    Includes index.
    ISBN 0-385-24874-1
ISBN 0-385-24875-X (lib. bdg.)
    1. Life—Origin—Juvenile literature.
[1. Life—Origin.] I. Title.
  QH325.B425 1990
577—dc20 89-35028 CIP AC
RL: 3.7
Text copyright © 1990 by Melvin Berger
Illustrations copyright © 1990 by Jerry
Lofaro
Printed in Italy
June 1991
First Edition

Introduction

You can see life all around you—people, grass, dogs, cats, flowers, trees, and much, much more.

Have you ever wondered how life first got started? How it all began?

To discover the origin of life, you can go on an imaginary trip—a trip back in time.

The first stop is 100,000 years ago. The people that you see on earth do not live in houses. Some look and act the way you do. Some are different.

At the next stop, 4 million years ago, you see the first creatures that resemble human beings.

When you reach 100 million years ago, there are no humans to be seen. The rulers of the earth are the huge dinosaurs.

The land is bare of all animals at 400 million years in the past. The only living beings are in the sea.

Now take a huge leap—back to 4 *billion* years ago. If you look very closely, you can see tiny bits of living matter forming in the sea. You are at the origin of life on earth!

But your trip does not end there. You zoom backward in time to 4.6 billion years ago and watch the planet earth being formed.

Finally you take off for the last part of your imaginary journey—all the way back to 15 billion years ago. You are now an eyewitness to the birth of the universe!

Let's start here. At the very beginning. The moment when time began. When the universe was born.

From the Big Bang —to the Formation of Earth

The time is 15 billion years ago. It is pitch-dark, freezing cold, and absolutely silent. There is nothing to be seen—no earth, sun, stars, or planets.

In this void—this empty space—only one thing exists. It is a tiny, superheavy, superhot speck. Yet, squeezed into this almost invisible point is *all* the matter and *all* the energy to form the *entire* universe!

No one knows where this little ball came from. Or how it got there. But some scientists think they do know what happened next. The speck suddenly burst apart with incredible force! The explosion was so tremendous that someone called it the "Big Bang." And the name stuck.

The Big Bang marks the birth of the universe. From that explosion have come all the stars and planets—and everything in, on, or between the heavenly bodies.

The force of the Big Bang sent out fantastic amounts of energy and huge numbers of tiny particles at incredibly high temperatures. As the particles hurtled out through space, some of them hooked together and became atoms, the basic building blocks of all matter.

By the time the universe was about 5 billion years old, the atoms had formed into huge masses of dust and gas that stretched across trillions of miles.

Within each massive cloud were smaller lumps that were spinning around at very high speeds. Gravity pulled the dust and gas within each lump closer and closer together.

In time, each lump became a separate star.

Soon there were perhaps 100 billion stars inside each big cloud, which is called a galaxy. And there were about 100 billion galaxies scattered throughout the heavens.

People call one of these galaxies the Milky Way. It is named for the cover of stars that can be seen toward the center of this galaxy. From earth it looks as if someone poured milk across the sky. The Milky Way galaxy is special in one way only: It is the galaxy in which we live.

Ten billion years after the Big Bang, a very ordinary star formed off to one side of the Milky Way galaxy. We call that star the sun.

After the sun formed, some particles of dust and gas were left whirling around. These little bits and pieces of matter kept bumping into each other. Some particles stuck together and formed bigger pieces. Somewhere around 5 billion years later, they became the big spinning balls that we call the planets. Nine planets travel around the sun. The earth is, of course, one of these planets. We believe it was formed about 4.6 billion years ago.

Every year scientists learn a little more about the far, far distant past. Perhaps one day someone—maybe you—will find new clues to help explain more about our mysterious beginnings.

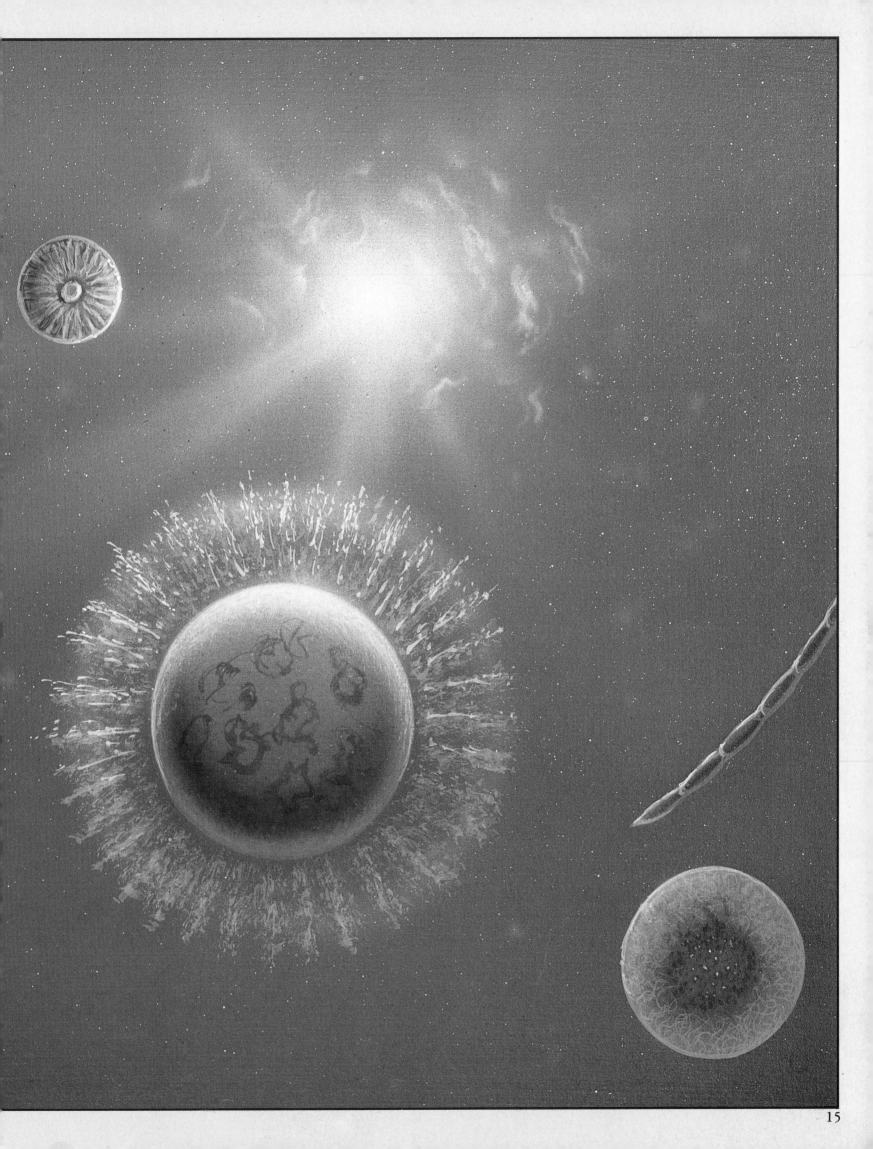

At the beginning, three main types of complex animals were especially common in the sea:

Sponges. Sponges sit on the ocean bottom without moving. Their bodies are little more than collections of separate cells that act as filters. As the water passes through, the sponges take out the food they need.

Jellyfish. They consist of a central cup or hollow, surrounded by long, armlike tentacles. As the jellyfish float along, their tentacles push any food they touch into the cup-shaped opening.

Flatworms. These early worms were basically hollow tubes through which water flowed. As the water moved along, the worms removed any food that was in the water. Most later forms of animals developed from the flatworm.

One very common group of animals that followed were the trilobites. Trilobites appeared on earth over 500 million years ago. They were sea animals with very hard

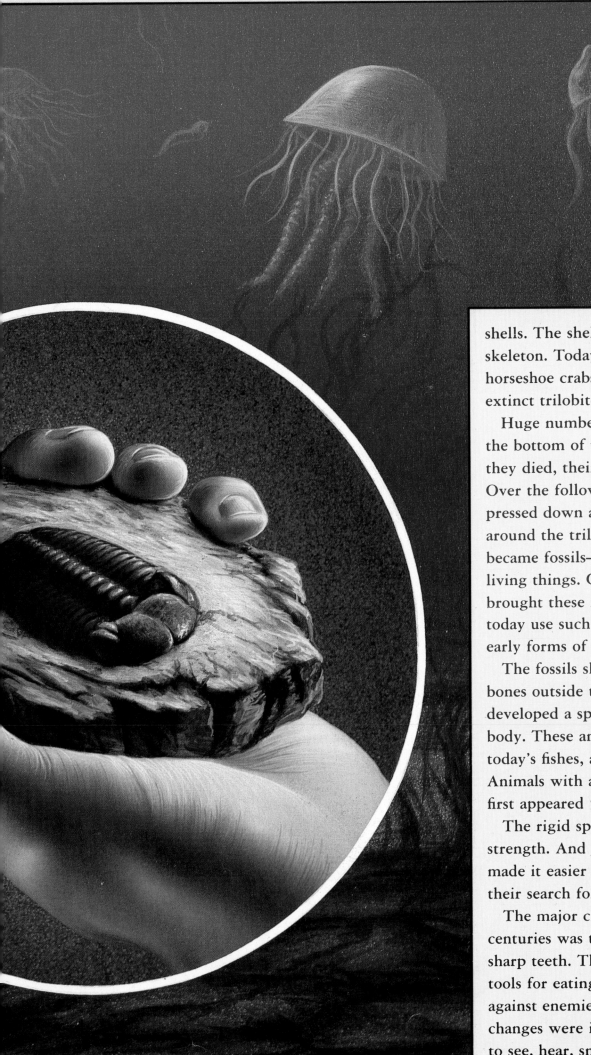

shells. The shell was actually the trilobite's skeleton. Today's shrimp, lobsters, and horseshoe crabs are distant relatives of the extinct trilobite.

Huge numbers of trilobites crawled along the bottom of the world's oceans. When they died, their bodies sank into the mud. Over the following centuries, layers of mud pressed down and hardened into rock around the trilobite shells. The trilobites became fossils—hardened remains of once-living things. Changes in the land eventually brought these rocks to the surface. Scientists today use such fossils to learn more about early forms of life.

The fossils show that not all animals had bones outside their body. Some animals developed a spine or backbone inside the body. These animals were the ancestors of today's fishes, amphibians, and mammals. Animals with a spine, called vertebrates, first appeared 500 million years ago.

The rigid spine gave the vertebrate added strength. And muscles attached to the spine made it easier for them to swim around in their search for food.

The major change in fishes over the centuries was the development of jaws and sharp teeth. They proved to be valuable tools for eating as well as powerful weapons against enemies. Among other helpful changes were improvements in their ability to see, hear, smell, and feel pressure. Some grew fins and a sleek shape that made it easier to speed through the water looking for food and escaping from danger.

From these early sea creatures developed all sorts of different kinds of fish. *Cheirolepis* (kye-ro-LEAP-is), one of the first of the modern-looking fish, swam in the oceans nearly 400 million years ago. For some reason, it died out long ago. But sharks, whose ancestry is just as old, have survived to the present day.

Meanwhile, some plants were beginning to move onto the land. It is believed that the first plant to make the move was

Cooksonia (cook-SO-nee-uh). *Cooksonia* lived about 430 million years ago. It could take in moisture from damp soil or rain. And since it could get carbon dioxide from the air, *Cooksonia* was actually able to live on land.

Cooksonia was a true pioneer. It was the first form of life to leave the sea and become land-based! As the ages passed, though, the earth grew green with many, many different types of plants.

The green plants—both in the sea and on land—were releasing gigantic amounts of oxygen into the atmosphere. Over the centuries, the bright sunlight was slowly changing some small amount of this oxygen into ozone, another form of oxygen.

The ozone floated up to form a layer about twenty miles above the earth. This layer became a protective shield. The ozone guarded living things on earth from the dangerous effects of the sun's ultraviolet rays.

Before there was an ozone layer, life could only exist in the seas. The water protected living things from the full force of the ultraviolet rays. But with an ozone layer, life could survive on land.

The first fishes to move out of the sea are called lobe-fins. They lived about 360 million years ago. The lobe-fins had gills

One of the biggest and heaviest dinosaurs—in fact among the biggest of all land animals—was *Brachiosaurus* (BRAK-ee-uh-SAWR-us), which means "arm lizard."

Like some of its relatives, *Brachiosaurus* was a vegetarian. It found plenty to eat in the swamps, where huge quantities of water plants grew. With so much food around, *Brachiosaurus* and the other plant eaters grew to immense size.

Brachiosaurus could reach up 40 feet—the height of a four-story building! At around 80 tons, it weighed approximately ten times as much as a full-grown elephant! Because of its great size, it could not run fast from its enemies. Then again, not many animals would want to tangle with a creature that weighs 160,000 pounds!

Few dinosaurs could compare to *Tyrannosaurus rex* (tye-ran-uh-SAWR-us reks), or "tyrant lizard, the king." *Tyrannosaurus rex* was indeed a king of beasts. Although it only weighed six tons or so, it stood about 20 feet tall and was 50 feet long.

The fierce-looking *Tyrannosaurus rex* had very powerful rear limbs. But its front limbs were surprisingly short and small. The double claws at the ends of these limbs seemed almost useless. Some experts think that *Tyrannosaurus* mostly used the claws to help it lie down or get up off the ground. Its huge head was 4 feet long and 3 feet deep. Lining its mouth were numerous sharp, curved teeth, up to 6 inches long.

Of course, not all dinosaurs were so large. The smallest was *Compsognathus* (komp-so-NAY-thus), "elegant jaw." Named for the delicate bones of its skull, this dinosaur was about the size of a chicken.

Reptiles were everywhere. They ruled the land and also the sea. *Ichthyosaurus* (ik-thee-uh-SAWR-us) and its close relatives were found in huge numbers in the water. With lungs, but no gills, they had to come to the surface of the water from time to time to breathe. *Ichthyosaurus* usually grew to be about 15 feet long, although some may have been as long as 40 feet.

from about 65 to 55 million years ago. This mammal was about the size and shape of a squirrel—though the two animals are not related. *Ptilodus* had a long tail and a sharp, pointed snout, and was covered with fur. A climbing animal, it probably spent much of its time in trees.

From the beginning of the Age of Mammals, mammals grew in great variety. Soon they became the major form of life on earth. *Hyracotherium* (Hi-rak-uh-THAIR-ee-um), the remote ancestor of today's horse, was one of these early forms.

Hyracotherium first appeared about 55 million years ago. No more than about 14

inches tall, it had a body shape somewhat like that of a modern greyhound. It was followed by a variety of ancestors of the horse, among them *Mesohippus* (mezz-oh-HIP-us), which was nearly twice as tall—about the size of a collie dog. The horse continued to develop until perhaps one million years ago when it reached the full 60-inch height of the modern horse, *Equus* (EK-wus).

Mammals of every size, shape, and weight have prowled the earth. *Baluchitherium* (bal-uh-ki-THAIR-ee-um), the largest of all land mammals, grazed on green plants and leaves about 25 or 30 million years ago. An early, hornless member of the rhinoceros

family, the giant *Baluchitherium* broke all size records, measuring 18 feet in height and 27 feet from head to tail. Its shoulders were as high as the head of a giraffe! When stretched to its full height, it could reach over 25 feet to get at the leaves on tall trees. This towering beast probably weighed 30 tons—three times as much as the very heaviest elephant!

There were many tiny mammals as well. The smallest of all is thought to have been the shrew. The primitive form of this mouselike mammal probably existed before the beginning of the Age of Mammals. Its modern descendant is the pygmy shrew, which is only about three inches long and weighs no more than a penny!

While almost all mammals live on land, a few, such as the whale and dolphin, returned to the sea. The blue whale is the largest of all mammals. As long as three buses (100 feet), this mammal weighs as much as eighty-five automobiles (140 tons)!

Curiously enough, almost no mammals took to the air. Only one, the bat, is truly able to fly.

A type of mammal that stands out from the others is the marsupials. Marsupials are animals with pouches who give birth to young before they are fully developed. Their reproductive systems are considered more primitive than those of the other mammals.

Kangaroos, for example, are born blind and without fur. Right after birth the newborn kangaroos clamber into their mother's pouch. Here they keep warm and feed on the mother's milk. After a few months they climb out and start to hop around on their own. When enemies approach, though, they scamper back into the pouch. The mother protects them until they can care for themselves. Two other well-known marsupials are the koala bear from Australia and the American opossum.

The duck-billed platypus and the spiny anteater are mammals that have even more primitive reproductive systems. They lay eggs instead of bearing their young live. When the eggs hatch, the young take milk from the mother, just like other mammals. The duckbill and anteater are good examples of mammals that haven't changed much over millions of years.

Among the many, many mammals that appeared after the time of the dinosaurs is one we call *Notharctus* (no-THARK-tus). Remains of *Notharctus* have been found in the present state of Wyoming. Here it lived in the trees of the forests that had covered that area.

Notharctus was small, about the size of a cat, with a pointed snout and a long, thin tail. Each limb had five "fingers" with which it grasped the branches as it jumped from tree to tree, munching on a diet of fruit, leaves, and insects.

Notharctus was special in one way only. It was a member of the group that contained the ancestor of today's human beings!

—to Modern Humans

The time is about 45 million years ago. The climate is mild throughout most of the world. Craggy mountains soar high above the earth's surface. Coal and oil have long since formed below the surface of the earth, along with such metals as iron, copper, silver, and gold. Great forests cover much of the face of the globe. The land, the seas, and the air all teem with many different forms of life.

Camels, horses, and rhinoceroses continue to change and become more numerous. The direct ancestors of dogs and cats make their first appearance. They are soon joined by pigs, mice, beavers, rabbits, and squirrels.

In the midst of this abundant life was *Notharctus* and similar small animals. They made their homes in the trees, moving among the leaves and branches.

After millions of years of change, though, *Notharctus* and its close relatives had become quite extraordinary. Their excellent eyesight and coordination allowed them to jump from branch to branch with ease. Living together in small groups, they were probably highly social. In many ways, they seemed smarter than most other animals. Today we call these animals and their later relatives "primates" from a Latin word that means "first."

The primates multiplied all over the world. They used all four limbs and the five long "fingers" on each limb to move gracefully through the trees. Soft, woolly fur covered their bodies, and most had long, bushy tails that helped their treetop acrobatics. Their nose and ears probably looked foxlike and they had big, round eyes.

Primates of this kind thrived for about 20 million years. In fact, some of their relatives can still be found today on the island of Madagascar.

Around 35 million years ago, a new kind of primate emerged. They are known as "higher primates." Among them was *Aegyptopithecus* (ee-jip-toh-PITH-eh-kus), or

"Egypt ape," an ancestor of the early apes, which appeared about 20 million years ago.

Pretty soon, though, the African climate began to change. Parts of the great forests gave way to woodlands. The new environment offered the inhabitants a different diet. One group of apes adapted well to harder foods, such as nuts and tubers, instead of the fruits that apes had eaten in the forests. From these woodland apes came the African apes—gorillas and chimpanzees.

At some point a line split off from the line leading to the African apes. A new kind of being emerged. In time, this line led to today's humans. Scientists still do not know exactly when this important development occurred. But it was probably around 7 to 10 million years ago.

One valuable clue to the development of human beings was found near the east coast of Africa in 1976. Scientists discovered a layer of rock with several footprints embedded in the rock. From their studies they realized that a huge volcano had erupted there about 3.5 million years ago. The ground had been covered with a layer of ash. Then it started to rain. The ash became thick, sloshy mud.

Three creatures that looked somewhat like today's humans had plodded through the heavy goo. The first one, large and heavy, had made deep footprints in the mud. Some say that a shorter, lighter companion had followed, stepping into the ready-made tracks. And, walking alongside, another creature had left a smaller trail.

Presently the rain stopped and the sun came out. The heat dried the mud. In time it became solid—but with the big and little footsteps permanently marked in the rock. These footsteps, the scientists realized, are some of the oldest traces of early human beings ever found on the face of the earth! And they are the first direct evidence of creatures who walked upright. Today we

call the creatures that made the prints australopithecines (awe-STRAY-low-PITH-uh-seenz), a word that means "southern apes."

Several equally exciting australopithecine discoveries have also been made in eastern Africa. Scientists unearthed the skeleton of a young girl who lived about 3 million years ago. It is the oldest humanlike skeleton ever found! The skeleton was given the name "Lucy." She was under four feet tall, weighed about 55 pounds, and had a much smaller brain than we do.

In some ways Lucy and the other australopithecines were apelike. They had short legs and long arms, large, jutting jaws, prominent brows, sloping foreheads, and

may have been covered with hair. But in other ways they were like humans. They walked on two legs, had small canine teeth like ours, and had a somewhat larger brain than the apes.

Australopithecines probably lived together in small bands, sharing their food and protecting one another from animals that might attack them. Vegetables made up most of their diet. Occasionally they would also eat a small animal they caught or nibble on the remains of a dead large animal. At night, tribe members may have slept in trees.

Remains of australopithecines have been found dating back to between 4 and 1 million years ago. But starting about 2 million years ago, there appeared a more humanlike being. We call it *Homo habilis*, meaning "able or skillful man." The name is often shortened to *H. habilis*.

H. habilis was the first toolmaker. Apes occasionally use a stick to get food from a place they cannot reach with their hands. But *H. habilis* actually shaped stones into tools. And they then used these tools as weapons, and to help prepare food. In addition to doing more things with his hands, *H. habilis* was probably able to outsmart his enemies, learn from his mistakes, and plan for the future.

H. habilis was replaced around 1.6 million years ago by *Homo erectus*, or *H. erectus*, which means "upright man." *H. erectus* was very different from *H. habilis*. He was taller —up to 6 feet instead of just over 4 feet— and heavier, with a more human face, and a bigger brain.

H. erectus also differed from modern people in a few ways. His skull was longer and lower. He had heavy brows over his eyes, a big jaw, and sloping chin. Still, *H. erectus* had many useful skills, including making and using well-shaped tools and perhaps hunting big game.

In December 1988, scientists reported that *H. erectus* had been using fire for cooking and to keep warm well over one million years ago. Cooking meat and certain vegetables made them more tender. And later on, the heat from fires made it possible for early people to live in colder lands.

H. erectus survived until about 300,000 years ago in the Far East. But in Europe about 150,000 years ago there appeared a new form called the Neanderthals. Neanderthals were more powerfully built than humans today. The Neanderthal skull had a more sloping forehead, a ridge over

the eyes, and a very large jaw and teeth. Their brain was larger than ours and had different proportions. But Neanderthals were not as smart as modern humans.

The world of the Neanderthals included many kinds of fish, amphibians, reptiles, birds, and mammals. Several of the mammals had grown to be quite large. Elephantlike woolly mammoths, mastodons, and woolly rhinoceroses wandered over the vast plains of Europe and Asia. A favorite target of Neanderthal hunters seems to have been the giant cave bear, a relative of the modern European brown bear.

Neanderthal remains found in Europe and Western Asia date from 150,000 to 30,000 years ago. Then the Neanderthals disappeared from those regions. Most scientists now believe that the line came to a dead end. The Neanderthals were probably either killed off or forced out by the arriving Cro-Magnons.

Cro-Magnons, who appeared about 35,000 years ago, were the first modern people to live in Europe. They were slimmer and taller than Neanderthals. In fact, give a Cro-Magnon a shave and a haircut and modern clothes, and no one would turn to stare at him walking down the street!

The Cro-Magnons lived only in western Europe. It was there that they produced the great art found in caves in France and Spain. But their culture faded with the last Ice Age, which came about 10,000 years before the present time.

Cro-Magnons, though, are only one type of modern humans. The entire group of modern humans is called *Homo sapiens*, or "wise men." *H. sapiens* probably first emerged in Africa at least 100,000 years ago. The oldest fossils were found in Israel in February 1988; they are believed to be 92,000 years old.

H. sapiens discovered how to grow food from seeds. They planted seeds in the spring and picked the plants in the fall. By storing the harvest, they had enough to eat all year long. This marked the birth of agriculture and farming.

Farming put an end to wandering and foraging. A steady food supply year after year allowed them to settle in one place. They built permanent homes.

The *H. sapiens* also learned how to tame and raise wild beasts instead of hunting them. How this improved their life! The people now had a year-round supply of meat—without depending on the luck of the hunters. They also used the skins for clothing and the bones for tools. And they put some large animals to work hauling heavy loads.

Now civilization advanced rapidly. The *H. sapiens* got better at growing plants and raising animals. They made new and improved tools of metal they dug from the earth. They developed arts, such as carving and jewelry-making. They began to understand nature better and used this knowledge to avoid danger. Step by step, they moved toward today's way of life.

The time of *H. sapiens*, of modern human beings on earth, is only a blink in the billions of years of the earth's history. When humans arrived, the earth had already gone through many changes, great and small. A rich and bountiful diversity of plant and animal life existed on every continent. The people flourished.

Humans now rule this planet—this ever-changing planet with its ever-changing life.

Will life continue to develop as it has in the past?

Will new forms of life appear and grow?

Will humans rule wisely?

What do you think?

ndex

About the Author

Melvin Berger is the author of over 100 books. He was elected to membership in the New York Academy of Sciences in 1983, and has been awarded prizes by the National Science Teachers Association, Children's Book Council, Library of Congress, National Council for the Social Studies, Child Study Association, and the New York Public Library. His books have been translated into fifteen languages, and prepared as filmstrips and audio tapes. Melvin Berger enjoys collecting antique microscopes and other old scientific instruments, and lives in Great Neck, New York, with his wife, Gilda.

About the Illustrator

After ruling out his initial career choices as a paleontologist, zoologist, baseball player, and Good Humor man (not necessarily in that order), Jerry Lofaro, who has been drawing since he could hold a pencil, combined his lifelong interests in dinosaurs, animals, fantasy, art history, and literature into a successful existence as an illustrator. Mostly self-taught, he received his formal art education at SUNY, New Paltz, and the Art Students League of New York.

Jerry Lofaro's art has been well represented in a number of shows at the Society of Illustrators, and has been in exhibitions touring Europe and Japan. Mr. Lofaro currently lives in New York City with his pet pterodactyl, Beak, and operates an art studio in SoHo.